WNBA
CHICAGO SKY
Mesirow
HAYES
AT&T
Mitchell Lane
PUBLISHERS
Joanne Mattern

Mitchell Lane
PUBLISHERS

mitchelllanepub.com

2001 SW 31st Avenue
Hallandale, FL 33009

First Edition, 2026.
Author: Joanne Mattern
Designer: Ed Morgan
Editor: Tammy Gagne

Series: WNBA
Title: Chicago Sky

Library bound ISBN: 979-8-89260-476-5
eBook ISBN: 979-8-89260-496-3

Photo credits: p. 5, 9, 11, 15, 21 newscom.com; p. 17 wikimedia; balance Alamy

CONTENTS

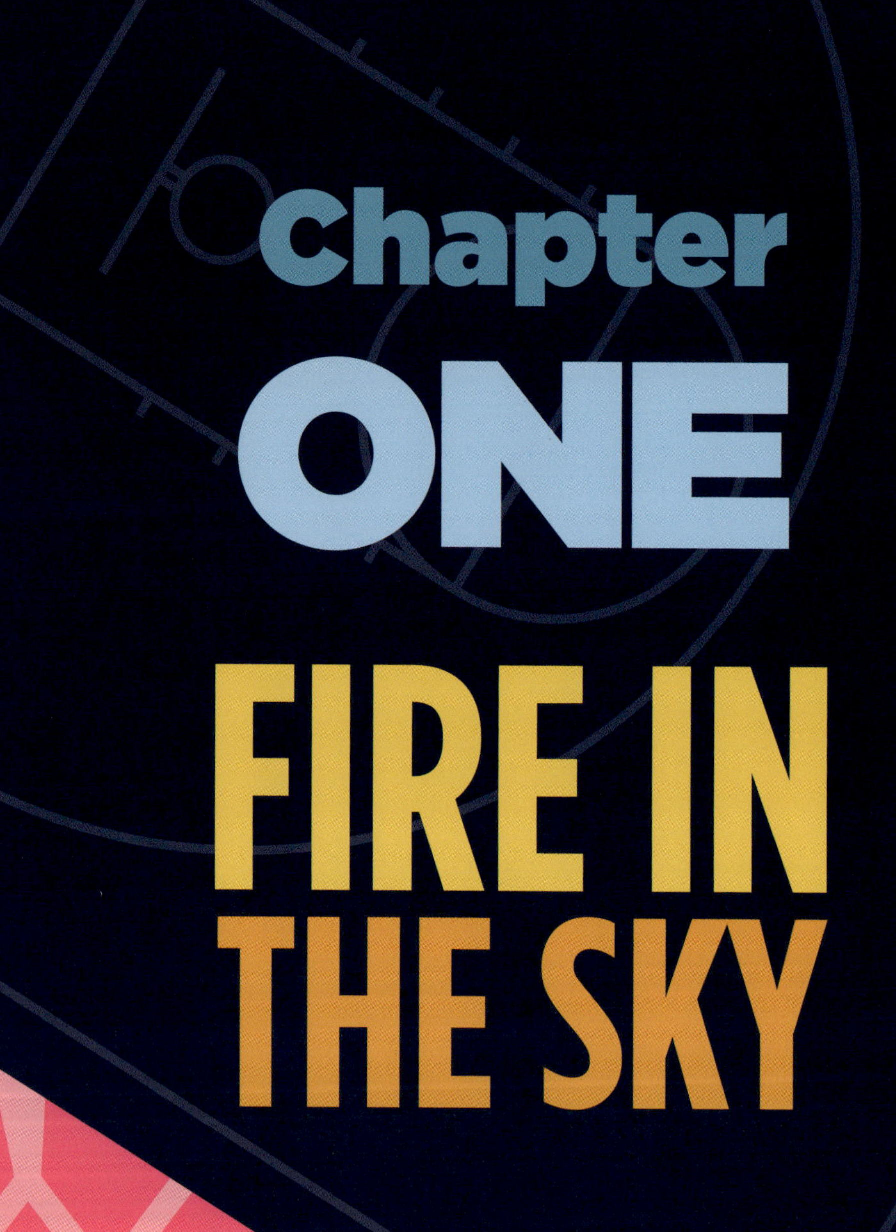

Chapter ONE
FIRE IN THE SKY

The Indiana Fever's NaLyssa Smith and the Chicago Sky's Kamilla Cardoso fight for a rebound during the game on June 23, 2024.

Excitement ran high as players from the Chicago Sky and the Indiana Fever took the court on June 23, 2024. Games between these rivals often resulted in back-and-forth play, close scores, and overtime periods. The Fever had beaten the Sky just a week before, so Sky fans were eager for this chance at **redemption**. Some fans had paid more than $350 for a ticket to the game.

CHAPTER ONE

Fans were also excited to see two top **rookies**, Sky's Angel Reese and Fever's Caitlin Clark, face off against each other. Those two players and their teams did not disappoint.

The Sky and the Fever were equally matched in the first half, with the lead changing eight times. Chicago exploded at the start of the second half, scoring nine points while the Fever were held scoreless. But Indiana came back strong as well, earning a 15-point lead in the third quarter. With a little more than six minutes to play in the fourth quarter, the Sky was behind with a score of 82–70.

Fire in the Sky

FAST FACT

The Chicago Sky selected Angel Reese as the seventh overall pick in the 2024 WNBA Draft.

That's when Angel Reese came alive. The powerful forward scored 10 points and snagged 5 **rebounds**. With just one minute left, the score was tied at 84–84. That's when Reese made a two-point **layup** to give the Sky the lead. After a few points from free throws by both teams, the Fever failed to score in the final seconds. The Sky won the game, 88–87, and Chicago fans erupted in cheers.

The night was a triumphant one for the Sky, and it was for Reese as well. She scored a career-high 25 points and grabbed 16 rebounds. It was the eighth straight game where Reese had achieved a **double-double**.

After the game, Reese told a reporter from ESPN, "I'm a dog," meaning that she doesn't back down from challenges. "You can't teach that. I'm [going to] go out and do whatever it takes to win every single night." That determination and fire is exactly what have made the Chicago Sky one of the hottest teams in the Women's National Basketball Association (WNBA).

Fire in the Sky

Angel Reese and NaLyssa Smith have a tense moment during the June 23, 2024 game between the Sky and the Fever.

REACHING NEW HEIGHTS

The Sky's Deanna Jackson moves past Murriel Page of the Los Angeles Sparks during a 2006 game.

The Chicago Sky are part of the WNBA. This league was created in 1997 as the women's version of the National Basketball Association (NBA), which has existed since 1946.

CHAPTER TWO

The WNBA began with eight teams, but Chicago was not one of them. The Sky was added to the league as an **expansion team** in the Eastern Conference Division in 2005, playing its first game the next year. The team's first season was a disaster. The Sky won just 5 of the 29 games the team played that first year.

The team improved over the next few seasons. In 2013, the Sky reached the WNBA playoffs for the first time with a record of 24–10. The team made it to the **semifinals** before losing to the Indiana Fever. The same thing happened in 2015.

It wasn't until 2021 that the Sky achieved the ultimate victory. Although the team's record that year was an even 16–16, it was enough to qualify the Sky for the playoffs. After advancing to the WNBA Finals, Chicago defeated the Phoenix Mercury three games to one. The Sky had finally won its first WNBA Championship.

Reaching New Heights

Azura Stevens lets out her emotions with a yell during a game between Chicago and Los Angeles.

FAST FACT

Chicago mayor Richard M. Daley named the team. He chose the word *Sky* because he thought it symbolized power and beauty.

CHAPTER TWO

Sky players expect the best from one another. "I like how we persevere," forward Cheyenne Parker said at the team's Media Day in 2019. "We push each other. The energy we bring is just an amazing feeling."

The Sky play at Wintrust Arena in the South Loop neighborhood of Chicago. The team is a vital part of Chicago's community, and the players enjoy giving back to their city. To achieve this, the team created the Sky Cares Foundation. Sky Cares benefits the people of Chicago by supporting a variety of **nonprofit** organizations. Since 2007, Sky Cares has held basketball academies for young basketball players. The organization also hosts programs focused on business skills, health care, social justice, and education. Sky team members are dedicated to improving the lives of their fans in many ways.

Reaching New Heights

Angel Reese, Chennedy Carter, and Lindsay Allen talk strategy from the sidelines during a game.

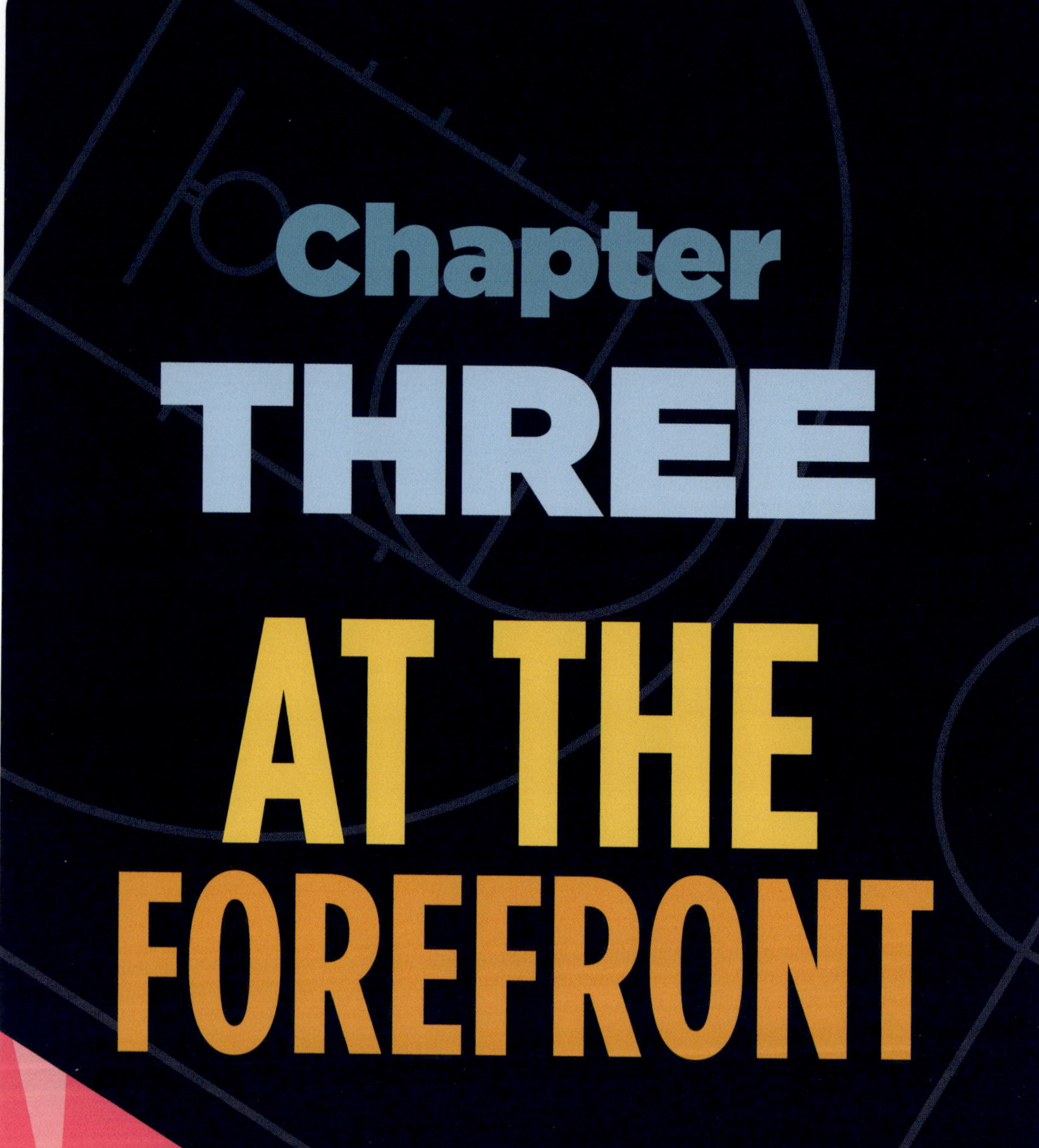

Chapter THREE

AT THE FOREFRONT

Dave Cowens was the Sky's first head coach.

In 2005, the Chicago Sky hired Dave Cowens as its first head coach and general manager. Cowens had been a star player for the Boston Celtics in the 1970s. However, he struggled as head coach and left the position at the end of the season.

CHAPTER THREE

The Sky did not get its first female head coach until 2010, when Dana "Pokey" Chatman took over the role. In 2013, Chatman led the Sky to the playoffs for the first time in the team's history. The Sky returned to the playoffs in 2014, 2015, and 2016 under her leadership. But each time, Chicago lost the championship to another team.

In October 2023, the Sky hired Teresa Weatherspoon as its eighth head coach. She began her new role at the start of the 2024 season. Weatherspoon had been a WNBA All-Star with the New York Liberty and Los Angeles Sparks. "We are thrilled to welcome Teresa Weatherspoon as the new head coach of the Chicago Sky," the team's co-owner and chairperson, Nadia Rawlinson, told the media. Rawlinson called Weatherspoon "the perfect choice to build on our championship culture and usher in an exciting new era."

At the Forefront

FAST FACT

Teresa Weatherspoon was named the WNBA Defensive Player of the Year in both 1997 and 1998.

CHAPTER THREE

Weatherspoon, who had been **inducted** into five different halls of fame, including the Naismith Basketball Hall of Fame and the Women's Basketball Hall of Fame, was equally pleased with her new job. "I can't wait to get to work!" she told the media.

Although Weatherspoon coached the team for just one season, she made a lasting impression on her players. Many were surprised when Weatherspoon was fired in 2024. Angel Reese told *People* that she was "heartbroken" that Weatherspoon was leaving.

Tyler Marsh took over as the head coach of the team ahead of the 2025 season. He previously spent time as an assistant coach in both the NBA and the WNBA. He was part of the Las Vegas Aces coaching staff that helped that team win back-to-back championships in 2022 and 2023.

At the Forefront

During her playing days, the New York Liberty's Teresa Weatherspoon moves the ball past an opponent.

Chapter FOUR

SKY SUPERSTARS

The Sky's Courtney Vandersloot prepares to shoot a layup.

The Sky has had some terrific players over the years. Courtney Vandersloot was part of the original team. She played twelve seasons in Chicago between 2011 and 2023, and she was part of the 2021 championship team. Vandersloot was nicknamed the Floor General because of her leadership abilities on the court.

CHAPTER FOUR

Kahleah Copper was another standout player for the Sky. She was named Most Valuable Player (MVP) for the finals in the team's 2021 championship. Copper led the team in scoring in 2022 and has more than 2,000 career points.

Chennedy Carter joined the Sky in 2024 and has proven to be a great **asset** to the team. In her first twelve games, she averaged 21.4 points and twice scored more than 30 points in a single game.

In 2024, Angel Reese became one of the Sky's top stars. The Sky chose the Louisiana State University player as its seventh pick in the 2024 WNBA Draft. Reese was named a WNBA All-Star in her rookie season and achieved the league record of most **consecutive** double-doubles with 15.

FAST FACT

In 2019, Courtney Vandersloot set the record for the most assists in a single season, with 300.

CHAPTER FOUR

After this accomplishment, Marina Mabrey praised her teammate to Yahoo Sports. Mabrey said, “She’s so consistent. She [kind of] just jumped in there . . . did all the dirty work, and now it’s all paying off for her.”

The Chicago Sky is a top WNBA team with some of the most talented and determined athletes in the league. Sky players continually step up to keep their winning culture thriving. When it comes to what this team from Chicago can do, they have proven that the sky’s the limit.

Sky Superstars

Marina Mabrey taps hands with teammates Alanna Smith and Dana Evans during a game.

GLOSSARY

asset
Something useful or valuable

consecutive
Directly following another instance

double-double
Achieving double digits in two categories, such as points and rebounds, in a single game

expansion team
A new team that is added to an existing league

inducted
Admitted into an organization

layup
A two-point shot taken from either side of the basket

nonprofit
Set up for a purpose other than making money

rebounds
Caught basketballs after missed shots

redemption
The act of making up for a previous defeat with a win

rookies
Athletes playing their first season as members of a professional sports team

semifinals
The round of a competition that is directly before the finals

SLAM DUNK WNBA TRIVIA

- Unlike many other WNBA teams, the Chicago Sky is an independent team. It is not connected to its hometown's NBA team, the Chicago Bulls.
- The Chicago Sky's mascot is Sky Guy. He is known as the team's biggest fan.
- The Sky Fly Kids are members of a Chicago acrobatics team that entertains fans during breaks at home games.
- Mayor Daley chose the team's colors. Blue symbolizes trustworthiness, red stands for passion, white is a sign of purity, black shows sophistication, yellow represents optimism, and green signifies growth and renewal.
- Elena Delle Donne won the WNBA MVP award in 2015 while playing for the Chicago Sky.
- In 2023, NBA superstar Dwyane Wade joined the Sky's ownership group.

FIND OUT MORE

IN PRINT

Barnas, Jo-Ann. *Courtney Vandersloot*. Focus Readers, 2022.

Davidson, B. Keith. *WNBA*. Crabtree Publishing, 2022.

Orr. Tamra B. *Indiana Fever*. Mitchell Lane Publishers, 2026.

ON THE INTERNET

***Chicago Sky*.**
https://sky.wnba.com.

"Chicago Sky," ***ESPN*****, n.d.**
www.espn.com/wnba/team/_/name/chi/chicago-sky.

"Chicago Sky," ***FOX Sports*****, n.d.**
www.foxsports.com/wnba/chicago-sky-team.

INDEX

About the Author

Joanne Mattern has loved basketball since she was a little girl shooting hoops in her driveway and playing at the local YMCA. She has written numerous nonfiction books for children, and sports biographies are among her favorites to research and write. Joanne lives in New York State with her family.